FIRST BASE FUNDAMENTALS

A Comprehensive Guide

Mastering First Base

From Fielding to Hitting

SKY BENSON

Table of Contents

Chapter 1: Fielding First...1

Proper footwork and glove work............................. 2

Handling throws and scooping balls.................... 7

Developing quick reflexes 11

Chapter 2: Holding Runners And Double Plays 15

Techniques for holding runners on 16

Working with the pitcher.................................. 21

Turning double plays from the first.................... 26

Plate discipline and pitch selection 30

Chapter 3: Offensive Powerhouse 33

Hitting for power and average............................. 34

Base running from first base.............................. 37

Chapter 4: The Resilient First Baseman 41

Building mental toughness 42

Staying focused.. 46

Leadership and Communication 50

Chapter 5: Physical Training and Nutrition..................55

Tailored workouts for first basemen 56

Injury prevention and staying healthy 58

Proper nutrition for peak performance............. 60

Chapter 6: Game Day Strategies..................................63

Pre-game routines and warm-ups............................64

Scouting the opponent 66

In-game adjustments 68

Closing Thoughts **71**

CHAPTER 1

FIELDING FIRST

Proper footwork and glove work

When you compare first base to the middle infield, where the action is nonstop, it might seem like a more relaxed position. But don't fall for it! The most important part of a good defense is a skilled first baseman. The anchor is you; you're the solid thing that grabs throws and stops runners. To deserve that title, you must be good at movement and glovework. You can go from being an "occupant" at first base to a defensive powerhouse by following these steps:

Basics of Footwork

It's essential to be quick on your feet. Think of yourself as a cat silently following its prey, ready to pounce at any moment. If you are a righty, put your right foot firmly on the bases inside corner. Leavers do the same thing with your left foot. This makes the base stable and lets you quickly turn in any direction. Don't stand still! Do a slight shuffle with your free foot (left foot for righties, right foot for lefties) before the pitch is thrown. You'll stay grounded and be ready to move based on where the ball is hit. As soon as the throw is made, the magic starts. Step back and forth slowly with your free foot facing the throw. By moving your body towards the ball this way, you set yourself up well to catch it. This is where the "first baseman stretch" comes in. Do you remember the cat example? This is your jump. As you take a step, keep your body low and stretch your glove hand outward. Do not spring for the ball. Instead, reach for it. With a strong base leg and a controlled stretch, you can achieve your farthest without losing your balance. You got it! What now? Bring the glove up to your chest and turn your body back towards the base. This ensures the catch is safe and lets you throw quickly to the next base if necessary.

Getting Good at the Glove

Be careful when you use your glove as a weapon. Here are some ways to make it work like an extra hand:

The Fit: An excellent first baseman's mitt is big, deep, and well-worn. It should feel good on your skin and let you trap throws without feeling like fighting a crocodile.

The Position in the Field: Hold your hand just below your belt buckle so the webbing faces the throw coming at you. This gives the infielder a big target and gives you room to catch throws that aren't on target.

"The Scoop": People who play first base love grounders. Here's the skinny (pardon the pun) on how to deal with them: Tilt your glove slightly lower to catch the ball as it hits the dirt. For a safe catch and a quick throw to get out, use your glove hand to scoop the ball up quickly and your throwing hand to squeeze it hard.

The Grab with One Hand: It might be necessary to use only one hand to catch high throws or throws right down the line. Hold on tight to your glove and point your fingers down. Get the ball stuck in the web and quickly throw it out before it bounces again.

It's important to communicate: Tell your infielders where you want the ball to go. When you say "glove!" or "chest!" they know which target to aim for. This makes it easier to catch and lowers the chance that someone will throw something crazy and miss you.

Making Practice Better

Ask a friend to help you throw tennis balls in different ways. Work on your smooth footwork, putting your glove in the right place, and making clean catches. In front of a mirror, make moves that look like you're throwing. This helps you picture where to put your feet and gloves correctly. Hit grounders towards you with a fungo bat or a throwing machine. To get better at aim and speed, practice scooping and throwing. Have a friend call out directions, like "left!", "right!" or "high!" and practice responding with the proper footwork and glove position. Don't forget that consistency is essential. It will get easier to do these things the more you do them. Pay attention to the pros! Watch how first basemen like Paul Goldschmidt and Freddie Freeman handle balls and strikes. Look at their steps, where they put their gloves, and how their bodies move overall. The best people can teach you a lot! You'll go from being a silent observer at first base to an active force if you learn how to use your feet and gloves properly.

The Art of the Stretch

If you do it right, the first baseman's stretch is beautiful. It lets you catch throws that look like they're just out of reach, turning mistakes into unique outs. Do not jump! Taking a slow, steady dip with your knees keeps your center of gravity low and gives you a safe place to stretch. Keep your glove hand under control while you extend it. It's harder to catch the ball, and it's more likely that the ball will pop out if the glove flaps around. Don't stretch too far to get a perfect throw. Try to guess where the ball will go and change your stretch to match. This gives you the most reach while keeping you as balanced as possible.

The Dance of the First Baseman

When throws go off target, footwork turns into an art form. Shuffle before the pitch? This is the shuffle step. It's even more critical when the throw goes wrong. You can change your position without losing your balance by taking a quick shuffle step toward the missed throw. Keep your eyes on the ball and backpedal slowly if you want your throws to go high. Keep your weight low and your hand outstretched to catch the high throw. Sometimes, you need to do a brave dive. Always put safety first! You should only try a diving catch if it is safe; the out is crucial. A well-done diving catch can change the game, but a careless dive can hurt someone.

The Art of the Scoop

You're good at grounders but getting good at the scoop takes work and skill. Tilt your glove downward to make a tube for the ball when throwing low. This creates more space, making catching the ball in the dirt easier. If the rollers are very slow, you might have to play barehanded. Put your gloved hand on the ball and catch it between your thumb and middle finger. Then, throw it quickly. Remember that this move is dangerous, so only do it when necessary.

The Double Play

It's beautiful to make a double play from first base. You, the shortstop, and the second baseman must work together perfectly. Your movement is essential when the ball is coming in. If the throw is on target, the player can quickly move to second base with a quick turn. If you must receive the ball first, use the shuffle step and the right way to position your body to catch and move quickly. Teams will know you want to turn the double play when you say "two!" loud and clear. These extra seconds give them time to get ready for the throw.

Getting Good at the Mental Game

Even though footwork and glovework are essential, don't forget how to play the game mentally. Keep your eyes on the ball. This may sound easy, but it's easy to get sidetracked by the players or the crowd. Pay close attention to the ball as it comes in from the pitcher's throw to your glove. Look at the batter, the situation, and the man on base. This information lets you guess where the ball will go and set yourself up properly. Don't be negative. Mistakes happen. Do not think about them too much. Get back on track, shake it off, and prepare for the next play. A good mood helps you stay in the game and sets the tone for your team.

You'll go from being a first baseman to a protective rock for your team by getting good at these skills and working on your mental game. Your chances of winning will increase if you work hard, practice, and love the game. Go out there and take over first base!

Handling throws and scooping balls

When you see how exciting shortstops and catchers' jobs are and how fastballs they handle, first base might seem like a more relaxed position. But don't fall for it! Someone good at first base is the unsung hero of the infield. They catch balls and keep runners from getting on base. Two essential skills are needed to master this role: how to use gloves and how to handle throws.

Your Trusted Weapon Gloves

Think of your glove as an extra hand that you can use as a tool to catch all kinds of throws. To make it a catching machine, do the following:

The Ideal Fit: It may seem straightforward, but a first baseman's mitt that is well-worn and comfortable is very important. It must be big and deep enough to hold throws without making you feel like you're fighting a bear. Imagine a nice, deep pocket that doesn't just block the ball but also grabs it.

Position on the pitch: Hold your hand just below your belt buckle so the webbing faces the throw coming at you. The infielder will have a big target, and you'll have some room to handle throws that aren't entirely on target. Picture it as a giant, open funnel where the ball can drop.

"The Scoop": First basemen are great at getting ground balls. Tilt your glove as the ball comes closer to get good at the scoop. In the process, a small pocket is made in the dirt that keeps the ball from spinning away. Think about how smooth and controlled it is to scoop ice cream.

The Grab with One Hand: A one-handed grab might be needed for high throws or ones that are screamed down the line. Hold on tight to your glove and point your fingers down. You must catch the ball in the web to win, not grab it with your hand. Picture seeing a butterfly. It's soft and safe.

Communication's essential: Do not be scared to call "throws"! At-bats know where you want the ball to go with a simple "glove!" or "chest!" This makes it easier to catch and lowers the chance that someone will throw something crazy and miss you.

Getting good at the incoming throw

It's all about being ready for throws and moving quickly for a first baseman. For a good throw, you need to move slowly and steadily. With your free foot, take a small step toward the throw. Then, extend your gloved hand a little and make the catch. Picture a cat jumping on a toy quickly but steadily. We all know that throws won't always go well. How you move your feet is essential here. You can move without losing your balance by taking a quick shuffle step toward the missed throw. Picture a light, steady dance step. It's essential to backpedal slowly for high throws and keep your eyes on the ball. Keep your weight low and your hand outstretched to catch the high throw. Imagine moving backward with ease, like a skilled ice skater. Sometimes, you have to do a daring dive to get them out. But don't forget safety first!

You should only try a diving catch if it is safe, and the out is crucial. A well-done diving catch can change the game, but a careless dive can hurt someone. Think of it as a measured risk, not a daredevil stunt.

Mastery of Ground Ball

Grounders are what first basemen do for a living, but getting good at them takes time and skill. If the rollers are very slow, you might have to play barehanded. Put your gloved hand on the ball and catch it between your thumb and middle finger. Then, throw it quickly. Remember that this move is dangerous, so only do it when necessary. Choose the last option instead of the first one. To turn a force play when a runner is on first, you must think quickly and do it smoothly. As soon as you catch the throw, move your throwing foot towards the base to make room for the throw to second. This makes it possible to throw quickly and accurately to get the out. Imagine being in charge of an orchestra and ensuring everyone is on the same page.

Making Practice Better

Get a friend and have them throw tennis balls in different directions. Work on your smooth footwork, putting your glove in the right place, and making clean catches. Do the following: Stand before a mirror and throw like you're doing it. This helps you picture where to put your feet and gloves correctly. As if you were a silent movie star, you are playing out the play without a ball. Hit grounders towards you with a fungo bat or a throwing machine. To get better at aim and speed, practice scooping and throwing. Picture yourself as a vacuum machine that picks up those grounders. Listen to a friend say, "Left!" "Right!" or "high!"

and practice responding with the proper footwork and hand position. In this way, you train your reactions to be ready for throws from any direction. Think of yourself as a cat responding quickly and decisively to a toy mouse. Pay attention to the pros! Watch how first basemen like Paul Goldschmidt and Freddie Freeman handle balls and strikes. Look at their steps, where they put their gloves, and how their bodies move overall. The best people can teach you a lot!

If you can master these skills, you'll be well on your way to becoming a first baseman, which makes your teammates feel confident and makes baserunners afraid. You must practice, work hard, and love the game to do well. Now, practice your skills and become the defensive rock your Team needs!

Developing quick reflexes

"For line drives."

The sound of the bat hitting the ball. There was a flash of a line drive going straight for first base. Adrenaline fills your body, making your heart beat faster. Everything comes down to your reactions at that very moment. Are you quick enough to grab that rocket and keep it out safe? Having lightning-fast reactions is a badge of honor when you play first base. They distinguish between a catch that gets attention and a mistake that makes you feel bad. To get better at those reactions and become a line-drive-eating machine, do the following:

Getting Your Tools Sharp

Your eyes are the way your instincts get to you. Work on getting better at seeing and following your eyes. Focusing on near-far movement and peripheral vision can help you catch the ball faster and follow it as it moves. Think of yourself as a hawk looking for its target, the ball. This is the most essential thing to catch. One way to improve your hand-eye coordination is to do drills where you catch tennis balls thrown at you from different directions, juggle, or use a coordination ladder. It's like getting your eyes and hands together like a perfect catching machine. Reactions happen faster when the base is strong. Doing exercises that strengthen your core and agility skills, like ladder drills and cone drills, will help you balance and move quickly in any direction. Think of yourself as a cat that is quick on its feet and ready to jump.

Getting your muscles to remember how to move

Now, let's get to the drills that will help you get those fast reflexes:

Drills with reaction balls: You should use these to train your reflexes. Get a reaction ball, which is a small ball that bounces in surprising ways. Get better at catching it after it hits the ground or a wall. You must act quickly and naturally because the bounces will be everywhere. Think of yourself as a boxer who has to be quick and alert to avoid getting hit.

Partner Throws: Ask a friend to throw tennis balls or other soft things at you from different directions and distances. Pay attention to moving your feet and hand quickly to grab the ball. The key is to talk to each other. Call out "high" or "low" to work on getting used to throwing at different heights. It's like playing catch with someone who can change their mind anytime, causing you to adapt on the spot.

Tennis Ball Machine: Making line shots can be fun with a tennis ball machine. Turn it up to high speed and work on your reaction time to the blur of balls coming at you while focusing on catching them with your glove. This exercise helps you feel like you're under pressure during a game. Imagine you are a goalie who must stop many penalty kicks. You have to stay focused and determined.

Practice makes perfect but with a twist.

Do not throw the tennis ball, but stand in front of a mirror and act like you can catch line shots. Pay attention to quick glove moves, changes in footwork, and body positioning. Imagine working on your reaction time while watching it happen slowly and changing your form. Use colored cones to mark areas or have a friend call out places ("left!", "right!"). Move your body and glove quickly to the spot that was given. This game teaches your brain to respond to what it sees without catching the ball first. Imagine you are a soldier who must follow orders quickly and correctly. You can play baseball by setting up a hitting tee or a pitching machine. You can have someone hit line shots at you or have a machine do it. This simulates the stress and uncertainty of a real game, which helps you use your skills to do well on the pitch. It's kind of like a practice run for the big game. Pay attention to the pros! Watch how first basemen like Pete Alonso and Anthony Rizzo handle line shots. Watch how they move their feet, hands, and bodies as a whole. The best people can teach you a lot!

The Mind Edge

Even though reflexes are critical, don't forget how powerful your mind is. Learn about the hitter, the pitcher, and the game. Based on the count, the batter's stance, and the pitcher's style, learn to guess where the ball will go. Imagine you are playing chess and have to guess what your opponent will do next. Train your mind always to keep the batter in mind during the pitch. Take your mind off other things and focus on responding to the ball when it hits the bat. Think of yourself as a laser beam focused on the goal (the ball) and not caring about anything else.: Things go wrong, even for the best people. Don't overthink about a catch you missed. Get your mind back on track, shake it off, and follow your instincts. A good mood helps you stay in the game and sets the tone for your team. Think of yourself as a superhero who quickly moves on to the next task after a minor setback.

By constantly working on these things—vision training, hand-eye coordination, balance and agility, mental focus, anticipation, and reflex drills—you'll get the lightning-fast reflexes you need to become a first baseman who loves line drives. As always, practice is essential. You can rely on your reactions more and more as you train them. Soon, it will be easy for you to catch line drives, turning what could have been a disaster into a highlight reel moment that makes everyone cheer for you. Get out there, work on your skills, and become the rock your team needs on defense!

CHAPTER 2

HOLDING RUNNERS AND DOUBLE PLAYS

Techniques for holding runners on

The fantastic plays shortstops make, or the fastball catchers handle, and the first base might seem like a place to watch. But a good first baseman is essential because they keep runners on first base from stealing bases. A lot of skill, planning, and even some lying is needed to master this art form, even though it might look easy. To become a master of the hold and keep runners on first, here are the methods you need to know:

The Way the Hold Works

To hold a runner on, you need to use the proper techniques. This is what you need to keep up with:

The Stand: Put your weight on the balls of your feet and stand a little away from the bag. This lets you quickly turn towards second or home plate if necessary. Think of yourself as a spring ready to move in any way.

The Glove: The glove strap should face the pitcher and be kept below your belt buckle. So, the pitcher has a big target to hit, and there's some room for throws that aren't on center. Think of it as a net that welcomes the ball when it comes in.

This is the message: Keep transparently talking to your starter. They only need to say "on" or "back" to know if the runner has a good lead or needs to be picked off. Imagine you are a quiet conductor who tells the pitcher what to do.

The Art of Lies

It's as demanding mentally as physically to hold on to a runner. Don't stare the runner down, but look them in the eye. Look at the hitter, the runner, and the pitcher in different ways. It makes the runner wonder what you'll do next, which makes them less likely to steal. Think of yourself as a poker player who keeps their cards close to their chest. If you time your fake throw right, it can throw off the runner. Use a quick arm movement and a shout of "two!" to act out throwing to second. The runner might think twice before retaking a big lead. It's like setting a trap for a mouse that doesn't know it's there. (But be careful not to use this too much!) Work with your pitcher to throw a surprise fastball every once in a while. This can catch a runner sleeping and could also see someone stealing. Imagine you are a magician pulling a rabbit out of a hat. Your move will surprise the runner.

This is the pickoff play.

The pickoff play is one way to stop bases from being stolen. Set up a signal with your pitcher that will let them know when you want to try to steal second base. It could be a slight nod or a look at second base. Think of yourself and your partner as spies sending each other secret texts. Focus on throwing quickly and accurately to second base when picking off a player. Aim for the catcher's mitt or a runner's hand or arm to tag them. Imagine that you are a shooter who can draw and fire very quickly. Don't just stand there after the throw! Return to the bag immediately if the runner tries to steal home. Move quickly from offense to defense like a well-oiled machine.

"Practice makes perfect, but with a twist.

As you practice your stance, glove placement, and communication calls, stand before a mirror and pretend to hold a runner on. This lets you look at your form and see where you can improve. Think about being a student player working on your form in front of a coach. A friend can play the role of a baserunner for you. You should work on hanging on, making fake throws, and talking to a phony pitcher. This gives you a safe place to practice lying and talking to people better. You can think of it as a role-playing activity to get used to holding a runner back and forth. Have a partner act out as the batter in a situation where runners are on base. You should work on stopping the runner, responding to the pitch, and, if necessary, trying to pick off the runner. This makes you feel like you're in a game and helps you use your skills to do well on the pitch. Imagine you are a soldier in charge of a training exercise before a real task. Pay attention to the pros! Watch how first basemen like Paul Goldschmidt and Freddie Freeman deal with runners on base. Look at their body language, how they try to trick you, and their pickoff efforts. You can learn a lot about how to keep runners away from you from the best.

The Mind Edge

It takes as much mental attention as physical skill to hold runners on. Look at how the other team's baserunner usually moves. How do you describe them if they're known for quick steals or big leads? This information helps you guess what they'll do next and act accordingly. Imagine you are a chess player trying to figure out how your opponent will move. Get used to the rhythm and delivery of the batter. Are you able to tell if the pitch will be fast or slow? You can respond faster to a steal attempt if you know the pitch, especially if it's a fastball that the runner might not see coming. Imagine that you are a baseball psychic who can see what will happen before it does. Stolen bases aren't the worst thing that could happen. Try not to give up. Think about what went wrong, change your strategy, and keep your mind on the next play. A good mood helps you stay in the game and sets the tone for your team. Think of yourself as a superhero who can bounce back from a loss and get ready to play on the next pitch. You'll go from being a passive observer to an active force at first base if you learn these techniques, strategies, and ways of thinking. If your team uses suitable holding methods and timed pickoff attempts, they will allow fewer stolen bases. This makes the other team's offense work harder and boosts the confidence of your pitchers. Holding runners on breaks up their flow and makes them more careful, called "defensive momentum." This strengthens the defense, stopping runs and making the other team think twice about taking risks on the base paths. When a first baseman regularly keeps runners on base, his teammates have faith in him. It shows you are dedicated to the defense and want to stop the other team's offense.

Keep things the same. You will find that these techniques are more accessible and more effective the more you do them. Soon, it will be easy for you to hold runners on, making your opponent mad and helping your team win. Improve your skills and become the protective rock that your team can count on!

Working with the pitcher

"On pickoff moves."

It might look like first base is all by itself, but what about handling grounders, catching throws, and holding runners on? On the other hand, a tremendous first baseman knows how to work with others, especially when planning pickoff moves with the coach. How can you and your pitcher work together like a machine to catch runners on base taking naps?

Putting Together the Bond

Pickoffs work best when you have a good working relationship with your pitcher. Talk to your start game and through the game. Talk about the baserunners' habits, when pickoffs might work best, and predetermined signs for starting a pickoff. Imagine that you and your partner are sending each other secret messages to trick the bad guy (the baserunner). It is essential to know how your pitcher throws the ball. Is their windup smooth or jerky? Do their arms change when they pitch? You can predict their throws and respond faster to pickoff tries if you know how they throw. Think of yourself as a conductor who has to read the rhythm of the pitcher's throw) to give the proper cu es (pickoff signs). Trust is needed for pickoff tries. You need to trust the pitcher to tag the runner correctly, and they need to trust you to throw the ball correctly. Talking comes from talking to others and doing things well. Imagine your friends building a trusting bridge across the diamond.

The Writing on the Sign

You must send the pitcher a slight, pre-planned signal to start a pickoff. These are some common ways to do things:

The Head Nod: An imperative nod towards the second base can be a warning. Not letting the batter or runner know about this is subtle. Picture yourself as an experienced player who sends a secret message to your partner across the table.

The Look: It co-worked to glance at the second base and then the pitcher. This works well if the pitcher looks at you while warming up. Imagine that the two of you are cops looking to ensure they have the right idea about the runner.

The Glove Squeeze: A quiet warning can be a light squeeze of your glove with your throwing. This needs to be practiced first and usually doesn't get mixed up with a way of catching. Imagine you are part of a secret society containing shakes of hidden messages.

How to Get Good at the Pickoff Play

After telling the player what to do, it's time to do it. Pay attention to these things:

The Rhythm: Being sneaky with your feet is important for first basemen. You can hide your next move with a quick shuffle to second base. The runner doesn't know if you'll throw or run back to tag them out because of this. Being quick doesn't mean you have to give up security. To move quickly, whether you need to make a precise throw or plant your feet to tag a daring runner, you need to stay balanced. Think of yourselves as quiet ninjas who move quickly and carefully to catch the runner off guard and get the out.

The Glove: Keep your glove as usual when picking off a ball. Moving the tag from your glove to your bare hand may make it easier. It's essential if you want to catch the baserunner sleeping.

Sometimes, a well-timed fake throw can work better than a real pickoff try. Use a quick arm movement and a shout of "two!" to act out throwing to second. The runner's timing is thrown off, so they delay before retaking a significant leakage, saying that you are an artist pupusa rabbit out of a hat. Your job is to surprise the runner with a move they didn't expect.

Making Practice Better

I do not think that pickoffs will be perfect right away. Practice ice pickoff throws and signs with your pitcher while in the bullpen. Start slowly and slowly speed up. Start slowly and slowly me. Think of yourself as an artist practicing a song to eliminate mistakes before the big show. There will be live batting practice. Pickoff should be a part of live batting practice. With runners on base and a batter at the plate, this lets you work on your communication and performance under pressure. Think of yourselves as fighters practicing in a real-life battleground. Video record your pickoff tries and go over them with your pitcher. Look at your movement, how you communicate, and how you throw. This helps you determine what needs to be changed and make the necessary changes. Think of yourself as detectives looking through security video to determine what went wrong with the pickoff. Pay attention to the pros! Watch how first basemen and catchers in the big leagues work with their pitchers on pickoff moves. Look at their...communication cues, sneaky movement, and how they throw. Keep an eye on how they change their pickoff tries depending on the count, the baserunner's habits, and the batter at the plate. Your pickoff game will improve if you learn from the best.

The Mind Game

The runner is most likely to be picked off when they have a big lead or seem afraid to steal. Don't use them too much, because that could alert the runner and make them more careful. Think of yourselves as generals who have to pick the right time to attack (the pickoff). Read the signs of a possible theft attempt. Is the person moving around? Is there a big lead? If you know the steal is coming, you can try to pick off the ball before the runner does, which increases your chances of success. Imagine that you can read minds and guess what the baserunner will do next. Pay attention to the game the whole time, even when no men are on base. You might miss a chance to pick off the ball if you lose focus. As shooters, you should always be on guard and ready to strike anytime. Building a solid working relationship with your pitcher, coming up with a straightforward way to communicate, and practicing your pickoff skills will make you two very good at catching runners in traffic. Pickoffs that work keep baserunners from stealing and put pressure on the other team's offense. The other team is kept on their toes, and your team has a tactical edge. A good pickoff can change the flow in your favor. Because it throws off the baserunner's flow, gets your team excited, and can lead to a crucial out. The other players feel good about themselves when the first baseman and pitcher work well together on pickoffs. It shows you are committed to working as a team and stopping the other team's offense.

It takes hard work, conversation, and a lot of practice to become a pickoff master. But the benefits are significant: you'll annoy baserunners, build defense momentum, and be a crucial part of your team's victory. Get out there, help your pitcher, and be the wall your team needs on defense!

Turning double plays from the first

The sound of the bat hitting the ball. A grounder that shoots down the line. Adrenaline makes your heart beat faster. It looks like there will be a double play, and as the first baseman, you are critical to this defense. It's beautiful to see teams work together and people with lightning-fast reactions pull off double plays. To go from being a passive first baseman to a double play master, do these things:

Basics of Footwork

A smooth double-play turn starts with how you move your feet. Learn these things:

Taking a Shot at the Bag: If you think there will be a double play, move to the inside of the first base bag a bit. This makes a clear path for the player (usually the shortstop) to throw the ball, and you can quickly step on the bag to get the first out. Imagine that you are in charge of traffic, and your job is to direct the play (the ball) to the bag (the goal).

This is the shuffle step: Moving your feet closer to the bag as the ball is hit. This controlled, short step brings you closer to the throw and lets you get to your glove faster. Think of yourselves as a well-oiled machine that moves precisely and quickly.

Where to Put the Glove: During a double play, keep your glove slightly lower than usual. This makes it easier to go from grabbing the ball to stepping on the bag for the first out. Since speed is critical, putting the glove lower makes the move faster.

It's essential to communicate.

A double play takes work from everyone. Talk with your friends about double plays before the game. Figure out who will call for the ball (usually the shortstop) and if there are any pre-set signs for different double plays. Imagine that you are soldiers making plans for the fight before it starts. Keep your eyes on the player who is throwing the ball. This lets them change how they throw based on where you are and where your hand is. Imagine that you and your partner are dancers who move in sync. If you need to, you can call for the ball out loud. A simple "Mine!" or "I got it!" can clarify things and ensure the move goes smoothly. Think of yourselves as teammates who quickly confirm what they will do before they do something complicated.

Getting Good at the Throw

A throw to second base for the second out is often part of turning a double play. Learn how to throw quickly and accurately. Work on having a solid core, a smooth arm swing, and a follow-through that takes you to second base. Picture yourself as a pitcher, throwing a fastball that always hits the mark. Work with your team to throw to second base. Pay attention to your footwork, arms, and how often you hit the goal. Doing things repeatedly is essential to make muscle memory and make throwing natural. Double-play drills are something you should do with your partners. Play through different situations, like ground balls to your right, backhand saves, etc. You can work on your movement, talking to people, and throwing all at the same time. Imagine that you are players practicing a scene, making sure that every move and line is perfect. Pay attention to the pros! Watch how first basemen like Paul Goldschmidt and Freddie Freeman handle double plays. Look at how they move, talk to others, and throw the ball. If you learn from the best, you can make your double play much more effective.

Keeping your mind sharp

Read the situation of the game. Does the player hit ground balls? Are there runners on base who can score? When you anticipate, you can set yourself up properly and prepare your mind for a possible double play. Imagine that you are a chess player trying to guess what your opponent will do next. Keep your mind on the game the whole time. Don't let lousy play or other things get in the way of your focus. A possible double play can be ruined by a single mistake. As shooters, you should always be on guard and ready to strike anytime. Show confidence when you're in a double play. Your good mood will motivate your teammates and make them believe the play can be made because of it. Imagine you are in charge of getting your team to work together towards a shared goal (turning the double play). You'll go from being a first baseman to a defensive game-changer if you learn these skills and become a double-play master. This is how your knowledge helps your team: Doing a double play right can turn the tide in your favor. It stops the other team from rallying, puts pressure on them, and boosts your team's spirit.

Imagine that you are firefighters putting out a fire to stop the possibility of harm before it gets out of hand. There are fewer chances to score. Double plays get rid of runners on base and prevent them from scoring. This is very important when the game is close and every out counts. You should think of yourselves as bouncers, keeping runners from entering your area (home plate). A double play works best when everyone works together. It shows how different people can work together to coordinate, communicate, and carry out plans. It brings people together and helps them remember that baseball is a team sport. Think of yourself as a band, each person doing their part to make a great song (the double play).

It takes hard work, practice, and a close bond with your friends to become a double-play master. But the benefits are significant: you can change the course of the game, stop the offense, and become an essential part of your team's defense success. To become the protective rock your team can count on, get out there and work on your skills!

Plate discipline and pitch selection

Picture yourself at bat while the pitcher comes up and the crowd roars. That's an exciting moment, but it's only the start for a good hitter. Plate discipline is the actual fight. You need to be able to tell the difference between good and bad pitches and only hit what you can handle. Here's how to improve this critical skill and become a pitch-picking master.

How to Say No

In plate discipline, you don't have to hit everything. It's about being patient and picky. When you swing at bad pitches, you lose essential strikes. You could lose in a two-strike count or, even worse, look stupid if you strike out. If you think of yourself as a fighter, you don't want to waste your valuable swings on pitches that aren't in the strike zone. Hitters who chase bad pitches become easy to guess. Pitchers can take advantage of this by throwing slow pitches or breaking balls, catching you off guard and making your touch weak. Imagine you are a poker player whose bold swings let other players know what you plan to do before you do it. It makes the pitcher work harder if you don't throw bad pitches. They might throw more strikes in the zone, which makes it more likely that you'll hit the ball hard. Picture yourself as a shooter waiting for the right animal (a good pitch) to appear.

Getting better at seeing

How can you tell the difference between a fastball that looks good and a curveball that looks good but isn't? Learn where the hit zone is. Based on their height and attitude, it's different for each batter. Think of it as a box around home plate where pitches must go for them to be called strikes. Imagine you are a fencer and know precisely where your target (the strike zone) is. Pay attention to how the player throws. Do they wind up differently for breaking balls and fastballs? Is there something wrong with the way they're delivering it? By looking at these small details, you can guess what kind of pitch is coming next. Imagine that you are a detective looking for clues about how the pitcher will hit the ball. Keep track of your at-bats and look back on them later. Look at your swing choices and the pitches you chased outside the strike zone. Self-reflection helps you understand your pitch better and learn from your mistakes. Imagine that you are a college athlete looking at old games to see what you can do better.

The Hit Language

Pitch picking doesn't happen by itself. Talk to your teacher about how you'll hit the ball before the game. Find your "swing zone" by looking at the other pitcher. This is the area where you feel most comfortable making a good impact. Picture yourselves as soldiers planning for war before going up against the enemy, who is the pitcher. Some batters use a thought-out word, like "fastball" or "curveball," to focus on the pitch they want to hit. This can help you concentrate and get ready. Think of yourself as a bowler quietly picturing the next pin hit. How you do things might change based on the count. You might be likelier to swing at a pitch just on the edge of being a strike when the count is complete. When the count is zero, you can be more careful. Think of yourself as a chess player who changes their plan based on what they see on the board (the count). Watch the greats! Observe how players like Ted Williams or Mike Trout approach the plate. Analyze their patience, pitch recognition skills, and how they change their swing based on the count. If you learn from the best, you can improve at hitting and choosing pitches.

Outside of the strike zone

Focusing on strikes is essential but remember that plate discipline is more than just telling them no. "Drawing Walks," You can walk and hit a base. If you make the pitcher throw strikes, you might get a walk, putting you on base and moving runners along without having to swing the bat. As a pitcher, picture yourself as a matador carefully controlling the bull until it makes a mistake and walks you. "Foul Tips" While foul tips can be annoying, a well-placed one can sometimes save a strike or throw off the pitcher's flow. Even a foul ball can be seen as a small win in this war of attrition. Think of yourself as a fighter who hits their opponent repeatedly with jabs (foul tips) to wear them down. You can go from being a passive swinger to a powerful one by improving plate control and pitch selection.

CHAPTER 3

Offensive Powerhouse

Hitting for power and average

How sweet it is to know how to hit. Power and grace are compared in a dance, and hitting the ball hard is compared to hitting the moon. Aspiring batters often don't know what to do: should they try to hit the ball hard every time, or should they focus on getting hits that keep the offense going? Thank goodness the answer isn't as clear-cut as it looks. Let's talk about how to balance power and average for a well-rounded way to hit.

This is "The Power Paradox"

There's no denying how good a home run is. Nothing is better than hitting a home run over the fence, clears the bases, and excites the crowd. Putting all of your power attention, though, can be harmful. This is why: You almost always get struck out when you go for the fence. Even if your team hits a few home runs here and there, a high strikeout rate slows down their offense. Think of yourself as a gambler who is always looking for a high-risk, high-reward bet that could often break you. Power hitters usually have trouble recognizing pitches outside their "power zone." This leaves them open to slow pitches and breaking balls, which can cause weak pop-ups or groundouts. You're like an angler who only has a net. You might catch the big fish but miss all the little ones. You might not change your swing depending on the game if you're a straight power hitter. Even if men are on base, they might still go for the home run instead of moving them along or hitting a sacrifice fly. Imagine that you are a fighter who can only use a cannon. You would not be very good at fighting close up.

"The Beauty of Being Average"

A steady hitter is very valuable, so don't forget that. They don't hit massive home runs, but they put the ball in play more often, which makes them useful for any team. Making touch repeatedly makes the pitcher work harder and increases the chances of getting runners on base. This can help score more runs, even if it's less powerful than a home run. Imagine that you are a persistent bug. You might not bite someone, but you'll be annoying for sure. Average batters know how important it is to hit the ball at the right moment. As runners move over, they can hit a line drive, a ground ball, or even a bunt for a sacrifice. Visualize that you are a skilled magician moving your teammates, who are runners, around the bases. You have an even better record if you have a good on-base percentage (OBP) and a high-hitting average. This includes walks, hits, and runs scored. You are a constant threat to the quarterback and a nightmare for the defense. You're like a sneaky ninja who always finds a way to get into base and cause trouble.

How to Find the Sweet Spot

The important thing is to find a good mix between strength and average. Build a strong core, a smooth bat swing, and the right way to move your weight when you hit. With this base, you can build power while still being in charge of your swing. Think of yourself as a machine whose parts are well-oiled and work together to make smooth and effective power. They not only work on hitting for power but also on hitting line drives and all fields. This gives you more ways to hit and makes you a more dangerous hitter. Take a mental picture of yourself as a painter who has more than one brush and method at their disposal. Figure out how to hit based on the situation. A base hit is enough sometimes. A well-placed fly ball for a double might be the better choice other times. Hit with thought and be able to adjust to the game. Imagine you are a chess player who plans your next move by looking at how your opponent (the pitcher) plays. Watch the greats! Look at how hitters like Mookie Betts and Joey Votto mix power and average. Look at how they hit the ball, approach the plate, and change how they hit depending on the scenario. To get better at hitting, you should learn from the best.

Becoming a well-rounded player takes hard work, practice, and game knowledge. By working on good skills, trying different ways to hit, and changing how you do things, you can improve your power and average, making you a formidable opponent. Be sure of yourself, step up, and show everyone what you can do.

Base running from first base

Picture yourself at first base, your heart racing and your eyes fixed on the pitcher. You're not just a bystander; you could be a tool, a baserunner ready to cause chaos on the defense. One exciting part of the game is stealing bases and putting pressure on the other team. The first base is where many great steals begin. Here's how to go from being a baserunner who stays put to a master at stealing bases:

What You Need to Know About the Lead

A good start from first base is the key to a successful steal.

What's the Distance? Hold on to a safe lead to jump to second base if you steal. How far you hit the ball will depend on how fast you are going and how long the pitcher throws. You are a runner staying close to the starting line (first base) but are ready to go when the gun goes off (the steal sign).

The Stand: Keep a little of your weight on the balls of your feet. This lets the runner reach second base faster when the steal sign is made. Imagine that you are a spring that is ready to be released.

Reading the Pitcher: Get a feel for the rhythm and movement of the pitcher. Are you able to tell if the pitch will be fast or slow?

You can get a better start on a steal try if you know the pitch. Imagine you are a detective looking at the pitcher's movements to figure out what they will do next.

The Art of Stealing

You must start well and jump quickly to steal a base. Watch your coach or teammate give you the pre-planned notice that the steal is on. This is usually a nod or a hand gesture. So as not to give the catcher or hitter away, this has to be very subtle. Imagine that you are hackers sending each other secret messages before the steal, which is a surprise attack. You should push off the bag hard and take a quick first step as soon as you get the warning. The catcher has less time to throw you out if you jump faster. Like a cheetah, you can quickly go from zero to sixty miles per hour. When you're getting close to second base, a backward slide keeps you safe from the tag and lets you get to the bag. To avoid getting hurt, make sure you know how to slide correctly. As a superhero, you should aim for the bag instead of the catcher as you dive into home plate to score the winning run.

How to Know When to Steal

It's not always a good idea to try to steal something. Here's how to pick the correct times to run from second base:

The Pitcher: It's easier to steal from pitchers who throw slowly or try to pick off many balls. Keep an eye out for times when the starter could be weak. As you wait for the right time to strike (the steal), picture yourself as a lion stalking its prey (the slow pitcher).

The Count: You could try to steal during a total count (3-2) or a no-ball count (0-0, 1-0). The catcher may not be as focused on getting you out as they are on the next pitch. Think of yourself as a chess player who takes advantage of your opponent's weaknesses (like the catcher's focus on the ball).

The Score: The state of the game is also essential. When the game is close, stealing a base can put the other team under much stress. However, if you're already far ahead, it might be a risky move. Think of yourselves as generals who plan their moves based on what they see on the battlefield, which is the game.

Bonus Tip: Pay attention to the pros! Watch how runners like Billy Hamilton and Rickey Henderson steal bases. Look at how they lead, when they jump, and how they slide. You can get much better at baserunning if you learn from the best.

The Mind Game

Watch what the player does with his body. Are they getting ready to throw to second? You can change your slide or fall to avoid the tag if you know what it is. Imagine you are a boxer who can see your opponent's punch coming and dodge it just in time. Stay focused on the game, even when you're not stealing. A bad jump or a mistake while running the bases can happen when you aren't paying attention. Think of yourself as a shooter who is always on guard and ready to shoot. On the basepaths, be bold, but know when to be careful. Don't try to steal when it's unsafe to do so. It's safer to be safe and steal another base later. Think of yourself as an intelligent player who knows when to fold (not steal) to get another chance at life.

Why an intelligent baserunner is helpful

You add a whole new level to your team's offense when you start to steal bases. Your skills can help everyone in these ways: Because a steal is always possible, the receiver and pitcher must be alert. This might throw off their balance, which could cause them to make mistakes or throw wild pitches. Think of yourself as gnats buzzing around the pitcher's head, making it hard for them to hit their spots. If you steal a base, you are only 90 feet from home plate and can score. This makes it more likely for your team to score runs and put pressure on the other team's scoreboard. Picture yourself as a hitter who just hit a double. You have everything you need to score the winning run. The odds are in your favor if you can pull off a good steal. It excites the crowd and your friends and throws off the other team's plan. Think of your team as an outsider that pulls off a surprise win. The stolen base is what sets off your victory.

It takes hard work, practice, and a deep knowledge of the game to become a base-stealing master. Work on your lead skill, spot the best time to steal, and keep your eye on the basepaths. If you can master these skills, you'll go from being a static first baseman to a moving, attacking weapon that makes the other team afraid and is very helpful to your team. To steal your way to a good season, get out there and work on your starts!

CHAPTER 4

THE RESILIENT FIRST BASEMAN

Building mental toughness

You have to think about baseball as well as move your body. Every sound—the bat's crack, the crowd's roar, and the stress of a close game—can test even the best player. That's where being mentally tough is useful. The invisible armor helps you handle stress, get back on your feet after a setback, and do your best when it means the most. To get mentally tough and become a better baseball player, do the following:

Mastering Your Attention

Focus is the first step to mental toughness. Close your eyes and picture yourself doing well. Imagine hitting a home run that wins the game, jumping to catch a ball, or throwing a strikeout. Visualization makes you more confident and helps you set your mind up for success. Think of yourself as a sculptor who shapes your mind to get what you want (the excellent play). Don't think about your mistakes or what might happen in the future. Pay attention to the pitch you're about to hit or the play you will make. Mindfulness practices, like taking deep breaths, can help you stay in the present moment. Imagine you are walking a tightrope. You need to keep your balance on the line (the present moment) instead of looking down at the net (past mistakes) or ahead at the other side (worries about the future). Noise from outside can make it hard to concentrate. Learn to tune out the noise around you, the people talking on the bench, and even your evil thoughts. Come up with a plan that helps you concentrate before the game. Imagine you are a musician who puts on noise-canceling headphones to get lost in the song (the game).

Getting used to failing

Have a growth attitude, which means you see mistakes as chances to learn. If you strike out, don't give up. Instead, consider what went wrong and use that information to improve your next at-bat. Imagine you are a scientist experimenting. The failed swing is just one piece of information that helps you improve your performance. Watch how skilled athletes deal with problems. Watch how they respond after getting struck out, making a mistake, or even losing. Take notes on their plans and ways of thinking. You should imagine being a student watching a master artist's work. The professionals are your teachers, and how they deal with problems is a valuable lesson. Take care of yourself. When you make a mistake, don't be hard on yourself. Everyone makes them. Learn new things and keep going. Think of yourself as a friend who gives you words of support at the end of a tough day. Be that friend to yourself.

Getting More Confident

For mental toughness, you need to have confidence. Positive mantras should be used instead of negative self-talk. You should tell yourself, "I can do this" or "I'm going to succeed." Talking positively to yourself boosts your confidence and helps you face difficulties with strength. Think of yourself as your biggest fan, always pulling for you to do well. Setting goals that you can reach and enjoying your successes can help you feel more confident. Start small and get stronger over time. Your faith in yourself will grow as you reach your goals. Imagine that you are a mountain climber. Each step (achieved goal) you take gets you closer to the top (peak performance). Visualization isn't just for making plays that go well. You can also use it to feel better about yourself. Picture yourself doing well when you're under a lot of stress. Imagine being calm during a tough at-bat or making a play that saves the game. This thought practice makes you feel more sure of yourself in real life. Do mindfulness activities like yoga or meditation. These methods can help you deal with stress, concentrate better, and learn to control your emotions, which are crucial to having a strong mind.

To Turn the Tide

Mental toughness isn't just about how well you do on your tests. Mentally tough players motivate their friends. Others can be inspired to do their best by their positive mood and unwavering focus. Think of yourself as a leader leading your crew through a storm. Your mental toughness keeps everyone focused on getting through it. There are good times and bad times in baseball. An emotionally challenging team can handle problems and get back on track after they happen. Think of yourself as a willow tree. When the wind blows, you bend, but you don't break. A mindset of mental toughness leads to success. It's easier to be successful when players believe in themselves and each other. Think of yourselves as a band that is playing in perfect harmony. Your focus and teamwork make a beautiful melody of success.

To become mentally tough, you have to go through a process. It takes hard work, knowing yourself, and a desire to improve. By using these techniques regularly, you'll strengthen your mind in ways that will help you deal with problems, stay focused when things get tough, and reach your full baseball-playing potential. Remember that the most complex person you'll ever fight is probably yourself. Your worries can stop you from playing your best, but you can become a real force on the diamond if you have a strong mind and never give up.

Staying focused

"And maintaining consistency."

Baseball is not a race; instead, it is a challenge. During the season, it is necessary to maintain a consistent level of effort and focus. If you want to reach your best potential, you must keep your focus and remain consistent throughout the game, whether attempting to stay interested over a long match or fighting a slump. Here are a few pointers to help you maintain your composure and perform at your highest level in every game:

Bringing the Mental Chatter Under Control

Quieting the noise within oneself is the first step towards achieving focus. You should establish a pre-game ritual that will put you in a concentrated frame of mind. By doing things like stretching and clearing your mind, listening to peaceful music, or visualizing achievement, you can do this. Imagine that you are an archer getting ready to take a shot; your routine will assist you in centering yourself and aiming for your target, allowing you to perform at your highest level. Meditation: Perform exercises that help you become more conscious, such as meditation or deep breathing. Utilizing these tactics can assist you in remaining present at the moment and preventing yourself from becoming preoccupied with thoughts about the past or the future. Imagine that you are a monk trying to acquire inner calm before entering the arena of competition, for example, the baseball pitch. Positive affirmations should be used in place of those negative self-doubts. Your capabilities and strengths should be brought to your attention. "I am focused and ready" or "I am capable of completing this task" can go a long way towards enhancing your self-confidence and remaining concentrated. Consider yourself to be your own best cheerleader and inspire yourself to keep moving forward by providing yourself with positive reinforcement.

Developing Habits That Are More Consistent

Baseball is a sport that incentivizes players who constantly put forth effort. Regular practice is essential to keep one's skill level steady over time. Instead of practicing whenever you feel like it, make it a habit to do so regularly every day, and set aside some time to improve your hitting, throwing, or fielding skills. Think of yourself as a sculptor continuously working to enhance their trade by participating in devoted practice sessions. You can better track your progress and maintain your motivation if you set attainable goals for yourself. To begin, begin with a small amount and gradually increase it. You will feel a sense of accomplishment and remain involved in the process to the extent that you successfully achieve your goals. Imagine you are a climber attempting to reach the pinnacle of your athletic career (your ultimate baseball goal) by creating milestones. After each game or practice session, you should take some time to evaluate how well you performed. You can find areas where you could improve and measure your progress over time with the help of this. Imagine that you are a scientist analyzing data; the data you use to enhance your procedures is the knowledge you gain from your performance in the game.

Keeping Your Attention While Playing

There is more to focus than just getting ready for the game. Noise from the outside world and the situation's stress can make concentrating difficult. Acquire the ability to shut out the conversation on the bench, the audience, and even your negative thoughts. Put yourself in the position of putting on noise-canceling headphones to completely submerge yourself in the game and eliminate any potential distractions. The ability to "visualize success" During the breaks between pitches or innings, give yourself a moment to imagine yourself performing well. Imagining yourself making a diving catch, hitting a line drive, or throwing a strike is a great visualization exercise. The mental rehearsal can assist you in maintaining your concentration and self-assurance. Imagine that you are performing the role of a film director, mentally preparing yourself to watch the perfect play unfold. Involve yourself in the activities of your teammates and coaches. Communicating your requirements and seeking support if your concentration is fading is essential. Teamwork encompasses the ability to maintain each other's concentration and motivation. To guarantee that everyone is on the same page, both emotionally and physically, it is essential to communicate clearly. Imagine that you are a band that is performing in perfect harmony.

You can achieve laser concentration and consistent performance by combining mental tactics with a dedication to constant practice. This will allow you to become an invaluable asset to your team while also allowing you to grow your skills. Continuous effort is required to make progress toward the goal of being a baseball player who is focused and consistent. You will witness the fruits of your labor on the field if you are patient and dedicated to your studies.

Leadership and communication

"With infielders."

At first base, you are a player and the infield leader. You are the quarterback who calls the plays and the strategist who coordinates the defense. So, imagine yourself in this role. Effective communication and leadership are required to have a well-oiled infield team. If you want to go from being a passive first baseman to a loud leader who guides your teammates to defensive domination, following these steps will help you make the transition:

The fundamental building blocks of communication

At the core of a powerful infield is the ability to communicate effectively. You make sure that everyone is on the same page; here is how you do it:

Alignment Before the Game: At the beginning of each game, choose the defensive alignments that will be used for various circumstances, such as hit and run, bunt defense, and so on. Talk with your teammates about these alignments so everyone knows their positions and duties. Imagine that you are a soldier waiting to receive their battle plan before hitting the field (the game).

Be familiar with your pitchers: Knowing your pitcher's tendencies cannot be overstated. Talk to them about what they are good at and could improve. You may need to modify your infield location by their tendency to toss many breaking balls against you. You should imagine that you are detectives analyzing your opponent's weaknesses (the batter) and adjusting your defense (the infield alignment) to take advantage of such shortcomings.

This is the signal system: Establish a signaling system that is both clear and concise for use in a variety of scenarios. Depending on the situation, this may entail verbal cues, hand signals, or a combination. The most important thing is to make things straightforward and consistent so everyone can immediately comprehend the message. Imagine for a moment that you are a member of a covert organization that uses a handshake or a secret word to establish recognition (the signal) before carrying out a complicated maneuver (the defensive play).

A Guide to the Art of Leadership

There is more to leadership than simply issuing commands. You may inspire and motivate your teammates by following these steps:

"Set an Example for Others:" Being the first person to hustle, the first person to yell for the ball, and the first person to support your teammates after a challenging play is essential. You will be the one to set the tone for the entire infield with your good energy. Imagine that you are the captain of a ship and that you are responsible for determining the path (an upbeat attitude) and guiding your crew (the infielders) through both favorable and unfavorable weather conditions (plays that are easy and difficult). The practice of recognizing and celebrating the achievements of your teammates is an example of positive reinforcement. When boosting morale, a simple gesture such as a pat on the back after a diving stop or a word of encouragement after a tough out may go a long way. Imagine you are members of a band praising each other's successful notes. Everyone is contributing to the beautiful symphony that is a faultless defensive play with their contributions.

An example of constructive criticism is: You should privately provide a team member with constructive criticism if you observe them struggling. Concentrate on finding answers rather than assigning blame. Your objective is to assist them in improving, not to bring them down. The two of you should consider yourselves as teammates working together to construct a house (their defensive skills). You should provide suggestions to strengthen the structure (their technique) without criticizing the effort that they are making.

Consideration of the Circumstances

Before the play ever takes place, an intelligent leader can predict it. Pay attention to the batter's stance, swing patterns, and baserunners on base. Utilizing this information, you can make an accurate prediction regarding the type of contact they may make and alter your positioning accordingly. Imagine that you are a chess player analyzing your opponent's next move (the batter) and will create and modify your strategy (infield location) to counteract it. Waiting until the last second to call for the ball is not a good idea.

Regarding ground balls hit between positions, it is imperative to communicate your intentions early on. Your colleagues will be able to alter their motions and better avoid collisions. Consider yourselves a well-rehearsed symphony to ensure a seamless and well-coordinated performance (the defensive play). Everyone is aware of their role and the cues that are expected of them. The situation in the game is subject to fast change. In light of the score, the number of outs, and the number of baserunners, you should be ready to modify your communication and placement. Imagine that you are firefighters adjusting their strategies in response to the severity and location of the fire (both of which constitute the offensive threat). Examine how renowned infielders such as Derek Jeter and Brooks Robinson led their teams and communicated with their teammates. Take note of their demeanor while playing, hand signals, and how they communicate with their teammates. Your leadership abilities might be considerably improved by gaining knowledge from superior individuals.

Advantages to having strong communication and leadership skills

Comprehensive communication reduces the likelihood of misunderstandings and mistakes. If both players know where they are positioned and what the play is, they can coordinate their defense better, resulting in fewer mistakes. Imagine that you are a well-oiled machine, with each component operating efficiently to generate a seamless outcome (a defensive play that is faultless). When a leader is strong, they instill confidence in their teammates. They can relax and concentrate on carrying out their plays because they are confident that they have someone trustworthy calling the shots. Imagine you are a Special Weapons and Tactics (SWAT) team member. The leader's confidence, which is yours, motivates the entire unit to perform at their highest level regardless of the circumstances. The outcome of a game can be determined by how well the infield is coordinated. To give your side a boost of energy and to take the wind out of the opponent's sails, you can perform a diving stop followed by a perfect throw to first base for an out. Consider yourselves to be a pack of wolves cooperating to hunt down their prey, which is the offensive momentum of the opposing team.

Speaking the loudest on the pitch is not a prerequisite for leadership. Developing a positive mindset, effective communication, and trust are essential. You can turn yourself from a first baseman into a field general by devoting yourself to continual growth. This will allow you to become the leader who orchestrates a defensive masterpiece and leads your team to victory. A great infield must begin with a solid leader at first base. This person should instill confidence, anticipate the play, and communicate effectively. Consequently, it is time to take the initiative, accept the responsibilities, and establish yourself as the quarterback of your infield!

CHAPTER 5

PHYSICAL TRAINING AND NUTRITION

Tailored workouts for first basemen

First basemen must balance quickness and power in their training program to make quick throws and explosive actions. A breakdown is as follows:

The base of the body

Lunges and lateral shuffles are two workouts that increase footwork and agility, essential for fielding ground balls and making rapid throws to other bases. Build lower body power for explosive moves such as digging throws to get runners out of the box. Box squats are an excellent exercise for this.

It is the upper body.

Rotator cuff and core strengthening: by performing these exercises, you can enhance your throwing mechanics and reduce the risk of injury. Dumbbell rows and chest presses are great exercises to build upper-body strength, which will help you throw more powerfully and maintain stability when fielding.

Music

Interval training helps improve stamina, which is necessary for maintaining focus throughout a long game. On the other hand,

Sprints enhance explosiveness, which is essential for making quick throws and covering ground on bunts.

Extra Credit

During reaction exercises, you will practice reacting to various fielding scenarios, including line drives and ground balls, to improve your ability to make decisions while on the pitch.

Adjust the weight, the number of sets, and the number of repetitions based on your current fitness level. Consistency and perfect form are essential to maximize the benefits of these workouts and develop into a well-rounded first baseman.

Injury prevention and staying healthy

You must be very active to play first base—dive for a ground ball and stretch for a high throw—but you also risk getting hurt. You'll get the most out of your time on the pitch and hit your full potential if you put injury prevention first and stay healthy. Here are some critical plans:

Pre-habilitation is very important:

Picture your body as a machine that works well. Maintenance is essential to keep things from breaking down.

Warm-up in a dynamic way: Set aside time for a dynamic warm-up exercise before every game or practice. Light cardio, mobility routines, and stretches that get your muscles moving and ready to move are all part of this. Think of yourself as a car engine. A good warm-up gets everything ready to work at its best.

Building Strength: Getting stronger in your core and upper body helps you throw with more power and control. Don't forget about your legs either; you need strong legs to be quick and agile on the pitch. Imagine that you are a building that is still being put together. A strong base (your core and legs) lets you build up your upper body strength for powerful throws.

Health of the Rotator Cuff and Shoulders: Throwers are more likely to hurt themselves in these places. As part of your workout routine, do activities that strengthen your rotator cuff to make it stronger and avoid future problems. As a superhero, a strong rotator cuff is your hidden weapon against getting hurt while throwing.

Pay attention to your body.

It's good to push yourself, but you should also know your boundaries. It takes time for your body to heal after doing hard work. Take rest days and get enough sleep so your muscles can heal and grow back. Imagine that you are running a race. Even the best runners need days off to avoid getting hurt or burned out. Staying hydrated is essential for good function and avoiding injuries. During the day, especially before, during, and after games and training, drink a lot of water. Think of yourself as a plant: you must stay hydrated to grow and do your best. Pain tells your body something. Don't leave it alone. Talk to a doctor or physical trainer if you have pain that won't go away. If you take care of accidents quickly, they might not turn into big problems. Imagine that you are a car with a warning light on. Ignoring the pain is the same as ignoring the light, which could cause more significant problems.

You'll spend more time on the pitch and avoid getting hurt if you make these habits a part of your daily life. Having a healthy first baseman is good for the team because they are good at defense, get regular playing time, and have a good mood. So put your health first, pay attention to your body, and enjoy becoming a well-rounded first baseman who doesn't get hurt!

Proper nutrition for peak performance

As a first baseman, you need to eat healthily. To play for a long time, you need steady energy, quick reflexes for throwing, and strength for moving quickly. If you want to be the best on the pitch, remember these things:

This is the Power Trio

Think of yourself as a powerful engine that gives you long-lasting energy to keep you alert while you catch, throw, and play the game. Whole grains, fruits, and veggies are good sources of complex carbs. You can think of them as fuel that burns slowly but keeps you going.

Protein is essential for maintaining strength and power for throws and quick moves because it helps build and repair muscle tissue. Chicken, fish, beans, eggs, and other lean foods are good choices for protein. You can think of them as the building blocks that keep your muscles strong and ready to go. Eat good fats like olive oil, nuts, avocados, and avocados. These give you steady energy and help keep your hormones healthy. They keep everything moving smoothly, like lubricants for your engine.

Pre-Game and Post-Game Meals

In the lead-up to the game, about two to three hours before the game, eat a healthy meal. Complex carbohydrates give you long-lasting energy, lean protein helps muscles stay strong, and healthy fats make you feel full. This food gives you all the nutrients you need for a long day at work (or the baseball pitch). In the 30 minutes after the game, eat a food high in protein and carbs to get your energy back. Getting your muscles to start healing helps them get better. Just like you need to refuel your car after a long trip, your body needs the right fuel to heal and prepare for the next game.

Water is Key

It's easy to lose water at baseball games. Drink a lot of water all day, especially before, during, and after games. An ideal amount of water to drink daily is two to three liters, about fifty to one hundred ounces. Imagine that you are a well-watered plant. Being adequately hydrated helps you do your best work and avoids getting tired.

Your body will be ready to perform at its best on the pitch if you focus on a balanced diet that includes complex carbs, lean protein, healthy fats, and plenty of water. Eating right is an investment in your sports success; it will help you dominate at first base and help your team win!

62

CHAPTER 6

GAME DAY STRATEGIES

Pre-game routines and warm-ups

Every great first baseman has a personalized set of practices that they do before a game to get their mind and body ready. Here are some ideas for what to do before a match:

Getting ready mentally

Picture yourself making important plays, like getting a line drive or throwing the ball perfectly across the field. Visualization boosts your confidence and gets your mind ready to do well. Think of yourself as a movie director who is planning for a perfect defensive performance. Get rid of the bad things! Say positive things to yourself instead of doubting yourself, like "I'm focused" or "I can make this play." Talking positively to yourself boosts your confidence and helps you play the game better. You could think of yourself as your best cheerleader, always encouraging yourself to improve.

Warm-up for the Body

Stretches that move your body, like squats, arm circles, and leg swings, will get your blood moving and loosen up your muscles. This prepares your body for the quick moves you'll need to make when you throw and field. Think of yourself as a well-oiled machine. Dynamic stretches make everything run smoothly.

Include drills that are similar to the way you move on the pitch. Get better at catching fly balls, throwing to different bases, and handling ground balls. This gets your body ready for the unique needs of first base. Think of yourself as a musician who warms up with scales before playing a complex piece (the game). Make sure you eat a regular schedule of meals before a game that will fuel your body without making you feel tired. Test things out to see what works best for you.

By including these things, you can make a pre-game routine that gets you emotionally and physically ready to dominate at first base. A routine before a game helps you concentrate and feel confident, which sets the stage for a good match.

Scouting the opponent

"And strategic planning."

It's not enough to catch throws as a first baseman; you have to know what the play will be before it happens. To get an edge over the other team, use scouting reports and strategy planning in the following ways:

Reports on Scouting

How does the batter stand? Is it closed or open? Do they pull the ball often, or does the hit line drive more? If you know their habits, you can change where you're standing to guess where the ball might be hit (ground ball, line drive, etc.). Imagine you are a spy looking at the hitter's habits to figure out what they will do next (the swing). You can figure out the best way to throw for outs by knowing how fast the baserunner moves. A slower runner might let you throw more efficiently, while a fast baserunner might need you to throw faster and more accurately. Imagine that you are a SWAT team. Knowing how fast the enemy is (the baserunner) lets you correctly plan your attack (the throw).

Planning strategically

Discuss defensive alignments with your coach and peers based on the scouting report. There are a few options here:

Moving the infield: For a pull hitter, you might move the infield a little to the pull side to get ready for a ground ball going that way. Imagine that you are a chess player who changes your pieces (the infielders) based on what your opponent (the batter) does.

Call for the Pitch: As a first baseman, you might have some say in which pitch is used if the case allows it. If you and your pitcher know what the batter is terrible at, you can choose a pitch they are less likely to hit hard. Imagine that you are a magician, and your opponent is the batter. Because you know their weaknesses, you can call for a ball they will have difficulty hitting.

You become more than just a first baseman when you use scouting reports and strategic planning. You become an information analyst and defense strategist, crucial to your team's success.

In-game adjustments

"And staying sharp."

Baseball is a game where things are constantly changing. What worked against one batter in the second inning might not work against another. Here's how to stay sharp and change how you play as the game goes on:

As I read the hitter

Did they change how they stood between pitches? I think they want to hit the ball the other way now. Plan for these changes and change where you're standing to reflect that. Think of yourself as a chameleon that changes its color (placement) to fit in with its surroundings (the hitter's habits). Would you say their swing is faster or slower now? This could mean that the pitch choice or swing type (bunt try, power swing) needs to be changed. You can guess what kind of touch they might make based on what you've seen. As a detective, you're looking at the hitter's (the suspect's) actions to figure out what they will do next (the swing).

Talk to each other and change.

Based on what you saw and the scouting report, tell your teacher or teammates that the infield should be moved to help you better guess which way the ball will hit. Imagine that you are a well-oiled machine. Sometimes, a small change (the shift) is all it takes to finish the job perfectly (catching the ball). Be loud and clear when other players are asking for throws. If you see a partner having trouble with a particular throw, help them and suggest a different one. Don't forget that good communication is essential for a successful defense. Think of yourselves as an orchestra. You are the director, and clear cues from you make sure that everyone is in sync and ready to make the play.

As a first baseman, you show how versatile you are by staying alert, changing your position, and talking to the other team members. You're not just responding to what's happening in the game; you're changing things ahead and becoming an essential part of your team's defensive plan.

CLOSING THOUGHTS

As you put this book down, take a deep breath and picture yourself as the defense leader and the first baseman on the pitch. You've improved your physical skills, learned to concentrate better and become more competent. You know how important it is to communicate, stay healthy, and eat right to work at your best. Becoming a tremendous first baseman is something you do for the rest of your life. Take on the difficulties, learn from your mistakes, and enjoy the things that go well. You can get better at what you do with every ground ball, throw, and out. Don't be afraid to try new things, ask teachers and mentors for help, and have fun! It's a beautiful game to watch baseball, and first base puts you right in the middle of the. Now that you know more, take charge of the infield, guess what will happen, and be the rock your team needs. The best first basemen aren't just good at baseball but also at leading, planning, and building a solid defense. Take the challenge, step up to the plate, and go out there and win!